Memoirs and Poems of a Misguided Junkie

CHARLES BATEMAN

WORKBOOK PRESS LLC
187 E Warm Springs Rd,
Suite B285, Las Vegas, NV 89119, USA

Website: https://workbookpress.com/
Hotline: 1-888-818-4856
Email: admin@workbookpress.com

Ordering Information:
Quantity sales. Special discounts are available on quantity purchases by corporations, associations, and others.
For details, contact the publisher at the address above.

Library of Congress Control Number:
ISBN-13:   978-1-956876-04-8 (Paperback Version)
              978-1-956876-05-5 (Digital Version)

REV. DATE: 11/05/2021

MEMOIRS AND POEMS

OF A

MISGUIDED JUNKIE

By Charles Bateman

ACKNOWLEDGEMENT

My deepest appreciation to....

All those who encouraged me and helped me in prayer, project, and financial support to bring this book to completion; to Chareese, a magnificent best friend of mine.

I want to thank also my brother; Robert and sister-in-law Denise, this book would not be complete without you.

Most importantly, my gratitude to the Lord and Savior Jesus for His grace and companionship during this project and the Holy Spirit's faithful guidance through this assignment.

Letter from The Author

I'm a 57-year old man who grew up in a very religious home. My father was a minister for 20 years and took his own life in 1982. I'm the youngest of three brothers and my sister died in 2009. I never graduated in high school but I have a GED.

I made a modest living as a metal fabricator for 14 years and now I'm retired. I live with my brother Robert and his wife Denise Bateman whom I love dearly. I have three dogs Ruger, Coppertone and Forest. I have a best friend whose name is Chareese whom I adore.

This is my second book, a sequel to my first book entitled "Twisted Spiritual Journey". And this is extraordinary because my life story is also included inside this book. I've been an addict for many years and this has been the darkest years of my life.

My journey of going back to the right path is really challenging but I was able to surpass them all by writing more poems and concentrating on good things about life. I hope you will enjoy and appreciate the stories and poems I've written.

May these poems bless you with healing, hope and humor. ♥

- Charlieboy

TABLE OF CONTENTS

PART I: MY LIFE STORY

PART II: Collection of My Poems Over the Years

PART I:

MY LIFE STORY

BEGINNING

YEARS

Hello, my full name is 'Charles Arthur Bateman' I was born on February 14 1964. I am the youngest of 5 children. My sister Debbie, my oldest brother Clark, then John and Robert. According to my siblings my father worked for Kodak films INC. He did very well there as we wanted for nothing. He however quit his job there to become an ordained minister. Life took on new adventures as we, meaning us boys were always up to mischief. My father was very strict as we had to be obedient or suffer the consequences. At the green old age of 12 I overdosed on tequila and I was bleeding internally.

My parents took me to the emergency where they pumped my stomach, I was pale and very greenish yellow and it was a week before I felt right again. From there I got into more trouble, I and a friend of mine made a decision to shoot rocks at cars passing by on a freeway below. I hit the windshield on a Porcha, the driver parked his car and gave chase, I was about a block ahead of my friend, I turned in time to see the guy punch Charlie in the face. It was an unwritten rule, keep running no matter what.

A few days past by and we were at it again. I met my friend Brian at the corner market across the street from my house. We then made our way down an alley way where we found a grower and we could see he had pot plants on his balcony. We grabbed a ladder from a house close by, I climbed the ladder and started throwing the plants to my partner in crime and we ran back to my house and hung them upside down for 5 to 7 days, this is to make the T.H.C. drain into the buds and leaves. And on we go!

HIGHSCHOOL YEARS

I attended Roosevelt JR high school, that school had many different gangs. There were Sherman, Lomas, Wilmas, Sky Liners, and Crips. I did my best to avoid them so I befriended a gang member named Pete Gestilum. we became very good friends, we smoked weed together, ditched classes, etc. Two years later I attended Castle Park High, in Chula Vista California. I quit in the middle of 10th grade as I grew tired of the gang life and moved in with my brother John and his wife Kathy.

I was struggling to get a job by then, but we finally found a solution as I entered job corp. It was in Moses Lake Washington. Once there I felt so glad to be on my own, checking out the variety of jobs at my disposal I picked electrical but I failed the course so I tried cement masonry, I did okay but still not for me. After two years in job corporation, I graduated category two and was paid two thousand dollars' readjustment money. I then bought a car, a baha bug. Then I got my teeth fixed and got a job at a super market, a job I absolutely hated and my boss Bill was his name fired me as I was to hungover to report to work

<u>EARLY 20'S</u>

As I grew into my earlier 20's I lived in San Diego California with my big brother Robert, we loved to drink and when I'm under the influence I tried meth for the very first time. I thought, wow! this is awesome and it became something I had to have every single day. It became apparent that I was going to lose my job but I just couldn't stop. Eventually I did lose my job, my apartment, my dignity, meth took everything from me. Now I've been clean for 3 years and my life is a good one as I no longer crave that unholy drug.

So in 1987 me and my brother packed what little we had and moved up here in Washington state, ironically it was my big brother John and his wife Kathy that took me in. I got a job as a bus boy at a restaurant called the Alamo. My troubles always caught up to me though as I ran a tab at the bar and brought home very little money. After a few months my sister-n-law left a letter for me saying she didn't want me there anymore. I was forced to leave and spend the night's couch surfing.

Soon, I ended up shacked up at a Quonset hut where there was no hot water, we had no food, I had no job and most days I went hungry. My levels of depression sky rocketed, then what I thought was a blessing to me my friend came home and we shot speedballs, heroin and cocaine, I was so grateful that I didn't at the time need to think about my fucked=up situation.

MIDLIFE CRISIS

So, the Quonset hut with all of its vices finally came to an end, that was 1988. Soon after all of that I got a job at the biggest coke dealers house making an embankment. We will call him Mr. X. So there I was hauling some pretty good sized rocks at his yard until it became a massive wall about a 10=12 pitch. On the other side of that was a manmade pond I built for him. He paid me in cocaine, about an eight ball a week. Then word got out that my brother, Chris Ingras and my bro's girlfriend Windy got jumped in Tacoma Washington, they took on 10 or 12 members, now' Chris is 6' 8" a very big and just as mean when need be.

They said they fought for 10 to 15 min. and they kicked some Spanish ass. Now it came to pass that Mr. X set them up, I was told that by my friend George Baker God rest his soul. So one day I was working changing the tires on a car for Mr. X and I had a 5th of tequila and got a little drunk and brave, I jumped him and in the heat of the moment he threw me down the embankment I made for him and then? I blacked out.

The next day I called him and he made it clear that he didn't want to see me around ever again! The next day George and a girl I had history with came to my pad and told me I pushed her into the fire place. He kissed me on the lips and then left. Mr. x put a green light on me but by the grace of God no one stepped up to the task. I know that I forgive Mr. x but' I don't like him at all. then in late of 1988 me, my brother Robert and Tom knight were all drinking, snorting coke and driving, when we got to the trailer park my bro parked in a ditch, we went inside and all of the sudden we heard voices, it was the cops and they were looking for us.

So, we waited for the cops to leave and when I thought it was all clear I told my bro. that I was going to get the truck out of the ditch. He pleaded with not to go out there, I said no its all good. So out I went and just as I was making progress in my rear view I saw a state trooper coming up on me. He asked me to step out of the truck, he could smell alcohol and asked, are you the one driving? just then I heard a man saying ' he was not the one it was his brother Robert, the man had it out for him because Windy left him to be with my bro.

I said no officer I was driving, so I was cuffed and went to jail. In jail I was lucky to get a job in the kitchen and was assigned to a dorm, not in population. I was sentenced to 90 days. So, after everything was said and done I got out of jail and with nowhere to go I asked George if I could stay with him. He let me stay there but as soon as Mr. x found out George told me to leave, I asked if I could stay till morning, he said yes. As I walked down the hall to my room I was covered in darkness. I randomly said God where can I go? at that moment my room was filled with a light that only could have come from God.

I was basking in a peace unlike anything I've ever felt before. I no longer was worried about where to go as I knew in my heart God was directing my path. I woke at 6am got dressed, grabbed my back pack and head out the door. I went to an apartment complex that I and my mother shared, it turned out that Chris and his wife were still there, I caught them just as they were moving away. I truly could feel God's powerful touch with every step I took. Chris and his wife Wendy drove me to the port Townsend ferry terminal and once it was across I called my brother Robert and he came, picked me up and brought me home.

<u>ADULTHOOD</u>

Once I made it home, my mother bought a 3-bedroom house with a guest house. There was me my brother Robert, my sister Debbie, her husband Harland and my subreno Paul. The following Saturday my big brother John had a talk with me, he said that if I did not accept Christ into my life, Christ meaning Jesus, I would be on my way to hell. I did not forget what happened in my room at George's place, the next day I went to church and accepted Jesus into my heart. My troubles didn't end there; they were just beginning.

I had a hard time giving up alcohol and soon something came over me, it was something I'd rather forget. I became very edgy and paranoid. I would hide anytime company came over as I just didn't want to be seen. This went on for about 5 or 6 months. My mom and big brother John checked me in to the third floor at Skagit Valley hospital where I stayed for two weeks. Finally, my best friend Dave took me before a pastor who read out of the bible then prayed for me. Finally, some progress, the very next day was a Tuesday my big brother John set up an interview with his boss Scott, I was hired, I was coming out of the darkness and into the light.

CURRENT LIFE AND BEYOND

After 3 years on the job I was married and thus became my new life. IT was very difficult. My wife at the time was constantly moving. She talked me in to moving to tri-cities where I landed a job as a sheet metal fabricator where I was making good money, my wife still wasn't satisfied so we bounce from Kennewick to Pasco to the other city which escapes my memory, oh! Richland is the name, anyway we bought a house just outside of Pasco. It was absolutely beautiful! it had fruit trees, an automated sprinkler system, a small shop. It was perfect for us a family of 7. Things were good, we were so spoiled, we had it all. Then after about 3 or 4 months my wife got the itch again, this time we moved to Bellingham Wash. First we had to sell our home, I was so bummed out but she kept on till no end.

My brother John is an h v a c. genius working for a company called

Bel-Aire htng n air. He clued me in to a job opening there for a fabricator. I met with the general manager for the job and he told me he would hire me and to wait for his call, I didn't wait, I just showed up the very next day dressed for the occasion and he just put me to work. It wasn't long before my wife wanted to move again so after 6 years of moving from house to house we finally split up.

BEING A FAMILY MAN-

BRIGHTEST & DARKEST YEARS

After my wife left me our daughter Crystala decided she wanted to live with me but it wasn't long before I spiraled out of control. One night me my neighbor and some other random guy were shooting meth and heroin and I had to go to work hung over and out of dope, I had to tell my employer that I was messing up really bad so in 1999 I checked into treatment at Sundown M Ranch, after the first week there I started mingling with the other people and my temper was calming down and started making friends. After treatment I was able to go back to my job as a journeymen sheet metal fabricator, making fittings for duct and furnaces. I had 10 months clean and sober, I got my own place and life was good, my quality of work was to the nut perfect.

However, I slowly started drinking after 10 months due to the large amounts of stress from my job. that is all I remember from that time. In 2002 I was injured on the job, my rotator cuff in my shoulder had a large tare in it, I eventually had 2 surgeries, one in 2003 then, one in 2004. I never went back to my job but my attorney was getting me paid and after 14 years I received a full pension and now? I'm retired. Now, at that time I was in a relationship with two kids and their mother, we both had an addiction to pain pills, meth, and alcohol. We paid our house payment once a month but soon? almost every dime we had went to pills and partying. We had epic fights! over drugs running out and the quarreling was nonstop day and night. This was how we lived for the longest time, 8 years.

<u>SURVIVING THE CHALLENGES</u>

In 2011, I think it was, my pension was given to me so I was able to retire early. I've been clean off of heroin for nine years, clean off of meth for over 3 years. I've been attending aa meetings, group sessions at a methadone clinic. I have a wonderful councilor who has been a very dynamic influence on me and my recovery.

I have an excellent mental health counselor who has observed my accomplishments over the past three years and I wouldn't think about having someone else as he is such a blessing to me so thank you Dan and Rachelle, you're the cow's milk.

Sincerely,

Charlieboy 🖤

PART II:

COLLECTION OF MY

POEMS OVER THE

YEARS

Hover

Do you feel like your drifting? like doves gliding on the breeze?
You feel so high as your kissing the sky and it brings you down
to your knees.
Here there is nothing to be afraid of, here the lion lays with
the lambs, how much love and respect do I dish out? 7.70 x70
grams.
For you see I love without limits, I 've learned to forgive every
wrong ,in our hearts we can be without hatred, we can all just
get along, In this world we will have trials, in this world we
will know pain, love each person as we want to be loved again,
again , and again.
I am going to do my part as my higher power shows me to do,
to give from the heart is a good place to start by giving all my
love to you.

<u>Only You</u>

I dream in earnest about the curves of your frame, tantalizing is
the scent of your well.
your hair is long and is like an ocean wave that beckons my
promise, you will never be nor should you ever be tamed as you
are young, you are wild and you are free to be the woman you
desire to be.
It's your free will that draws me in as many a men have tried
but failed to see your mind, your heart and your soul. that is my
wealth, my passion and my birth right to love only you

<u>My World</u>

In the deepest, darkest of night you have invaded my dream.
Your ruby lips are full , beautiful pillows that when kissed by
them I am set on fire.
You must know that in that heat, that one simple act my blood
boils over consumed by your juices forcing me to swallow every
drop.
No other woman could take your place for you have branded
my ass with your name and I will always be ready to make
sweet, hard love with no reservations, for I long to inhale every
part of you , my lover, my mate, my world.
I don't actually have a woman in my life right now but if I did it
would have to be real, I can dream right?

No more

Telling my story is so hard to do, the pain is so hard to bare, there is much I confess was a terrible mess, to what of it can I compare? there is so much you see?
so unsettled in me I would look out my window and stare. I had my first drink at age seven, I smoked my first bong hit at nine, at age fourteen I overdosed on tequila
I drank so much that I nearly died. From there my life seemed so confusing, I hardly knew what to do with my time, so I just kept on using to forget about this life of mine.
I lost every job that they gave me, I drank until I was a corpse, once I even went to Las Vegas and bet on a high loosing horse.
In the eighties things just got harder as I got addicted to meth, my skin literally crawled as I stood by the wall and I prayed for a slow painful death.
Now I've put it behind me, now I'm finally clean, it's been three years in the making with no more of that life for me.

A Measure

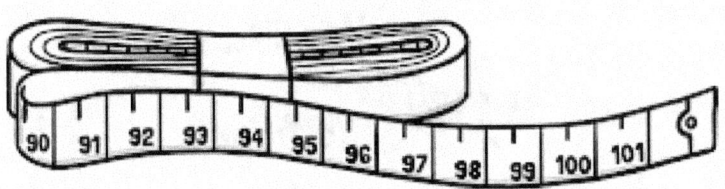

Time is so valuable but time we can't buy , no matter how bad
we want it nor how hard we try .
So , make the best of time we do have cause it ain't no joke ,
you'll see the very best intentions just go up in smoke.
Don't live for tomorrow for we just have today , watch what
you do and the words that you say .
Think on the present , learn from the past don't dwell on a
memory and the shadow it casts .
Give it your all in all that you do , help those in need
that have it harder than you.
For this tiny moment maybe all that we get , for I have faith in
you and I'm willing to bet ,
With your time use wisdom because one thing I see?
Is that we are warriors and so happy to be.

Some days

Some days are depressing and the air is so thick , I search in the dark cause I can't light my wick

I choose to be a lone wolf but even lone wolves cry , they will send a tingle down the back of your spine .

Who must I talk to ? doe's anyone know ? I show up a looser for the end of the show.

I dwell on my self-pity it's all that I own , I sat for hours by the living room phone . Hoping that someone , anyone at all , would pay me a visit but my hope was too small .

So here I sit on the edge of my bed with thoughts of a better life swimming round in my head .

Someday it may happen, I may win the fight, that's all I can tell you, I bid you all a good night.

For some

Here I yearn for the one that I love, she has the wings of
an angel, she is as white as a dove. In the moon light she
glistens, her form is so true, her eyes are like sapphires with a
bright yellow hue. In her absence I beckoned her to please hear
my cry, when she doesn't answer it brings a tear to my eye.
So here I do ponder a promise I swore, that I would be waiting
at the foot of her door. For true love is rare, it seldom does
come, not for the masses but only for some.

Keep it Short and Sweet

Keep it simple

The way we treat each other, the words we say undone, giving
way to hurtful acts fearing the next words yet to come.
Your heartless insults resonate I hear them loud and clear, keep
your comments to yourself for they aren't welcome here.
For I don't need your approval your validation weak, your
presence unacknowledged, the insults when you speak.

<u>Charity</u>

CHARITY

I think of the people whose lives have been wrecked, to offer
them kindness with some love and respect. Look past their
failures as God see's the heart, that is sufficient and a good place
to start.

Remember God's greatest and most humble command, to
love thy neighbor when you offer your hand. A voice to speak
wisely, with an ear listen close, give what is needed and
yearned for the most.

From God Above

To God the father, to Jesus the son, he conquered death when he said it is done.
On his shoulders he took the sins of the world, for every man and woman every boy every girl.
After three days he rose from the dead, ascending to heaven with a Crown of gold on his head.
So, give the glory to Jesus, the praise give to God, show mercy towards your children, give them love not the rod.
Please love thy neighbor as you want to be loved, for every good thing is from God up above.

Eighteen Tears

I'll cry eighteen tears for you, I hate what I had to do to make
your life a little better. I hope you can forgive me, be happy
and outlive me, just know I mean every letter. You were my
sunshine, my light in the dark times, every day without you
makes me so empty. We were always so close, what I miss the
most, is the time we shared and we had plenty. I pray God will
bring you, before I'm worn like an old shoe, my love for you
only grows stronger. I'll never give up, nor will I drink from that
old cup, in my heart I know it won't be much longer.
I wrote this for my daughter Raequel Schmidt, 10 years ago I
gave her up to be adopted.
Now, she is 18 years old and now will reside with me.

Inspire

INSPIRE

I will never judge you with hatred or disdain,
I will never cause you strife that you may in peace
remain.
God forbid anyone insult you or clip your angel wings ,
I will stand in awe of you and the wonder that you bring.
I will knock down all the walls that have made you poor
I will help you take the leap and watch your spirit soar
for you I wrote this insignificant poem to tell you of your worth
you will have your portion and your cup , you will be my friend
secure.
you have value and worth, don't let anyone say you don't new
poem

Sad but True

Tens beyond millions wait to decide, with nowhere to run to
and no place to hide.

Get out of the darkness, step into the light, do not be ashamed
of what's good and what's right.

I understand you are hurting, with sorrow's and more, look into
your heart till you come to a door.

Open it wide and let courage come in, get rid of your guilt and
say goodbye to your sin.

This was that something that only he could do, he paid with his
life and the blood that they drew.

Now there is mercy as he forgives every wrong, no man
suffered like he as the nails were so strong.

So, it is completed if we only believe, he is the salvation for you
and for me.

Wicked Heart Lives

The wicked heart is not from above, never has it felt the warmth
of unconditional love.
It doesn't know mercy as it has only known hate, it did not feed
the poor man that begged at its gate.
This heart is evil in every way, selfish and greedy, unkind to
this day.
How does this happen? it's way is unclear, in place of your
courage it will feed on your fear. Steer away from this one that
brings only death, it will take all the good as it drawls its last
breath.
These are my feelings in all the years that I've known, this heart
is hard mostly made out of stone.
This is what happens as it never forgives, the good heart dies
and the wicked heart lives

<u>Time</u>

I look at all the years gone by their substance gulfed in time.
Days are in the mix with all of their tricks the weeks and months
sublime.
With all of the time that I've been given I'm grateful for it all, for
a new chance at life with all of its strife even when I take a fall.
You see time is so precious the millionaires would give it all for
just one more drop, I'm sorry to say that time can't be paid it
always has to come to a stop.
So, while we're all here stay true to what's dear and when time
is over for you, I pray no regret I haven't had any yet and part of
me will be glad to be through.
I wrote this poem thinking about what is really important in life
and for me it is time, the poem tells the rest.

An Ode to Lori

A memory on a soft still breeze travels through the tall pine
trees, a whisper spoken in the dawning night.
I long to feel your dark long hair the look you give when I catch
you stare my love for you the only thing was right.
I make this solemn holy vow to give my heart to you right now,
I will only take that which I give.
The gentle waters calm your fears as I collect your coming tears
with righteous prayers to help you really live.
For you I've found a brand new love sent to me from God above
amazing is this overwhelming gift.
I beckon for a blessing to you in all you'll ever say or do, each
burden comes and I shall gladly lift.
This poem was written with complete conviction as I now
realize I lost my one true love.

The Used to Be

Luis J Bookman what did you do? you cheated death, now he's a coming for you.

Hide in the mountains, go climb up a tree, I'm sorry Mr. Bookman but you'll never be free.

You have been dead now for many a day. You lie in your coffin with not much to say.

You think on the matter, where did I go wrong? Lord please forgive me? and I'll sang you a song.

Then a light shown from heaven and blew off his lid, the Lord said I've been forgiving you since you were a kid.

Luis J Bookman was warm in the light, a voice said we're leaving post haste tonight.

The Lord said to Luis, you have never lost faith, you stayed true to your calling, saved by my grace. The Lord said "my child" your journey is through.

There'll be 'no more time in the use to be' for you.

Written for a character that dwelled in my mind, now? he's in heaven where I'm still waiting to be.

Truly Needed

Bright was the hour, the feeling was calm, the peace that I
cannot describe.
Gone was the fear and the doubt that followed as they were
replaced with courage and a determination, to remain free from
demons that brought them to me at no extra charge.
Today I will walk tall in moments I might feel defeated.
For I shall always remain free and will not allow myself to be a
man held in bondage for those chains are forever broken with a
holy promise.
My body can be cut and if so in time it will heal, my feelings
may suffer from undeserved insults and if so I shall rise above it
for all things that come also they shall pass away.
If my enemy brings me a threat I will bring him a blessing, if he
meets me with hate I shall return it with love, for in the end love
covers multitudes of these things aforementioned here. Love is
one of many things we need.

<u>Light</u>

I wake in a star lit sky, praying for a rainy night.
As I wonder I imagine there, peace exists where people care.
Living in a foreign land, singing songs as we all stand. Living
free and unafraid, know the heavy debt was paid.
Longing for undying love, came to me from God above. Basking
in the warmth sublime, painting words to make them rhyme.
I can sense my angel's watching down, you'll find them too
where God abounds. Thunder crashing, lightning's flash,
embers burning turn to ash. I hope that you find these things
too, as I also see the light in you.
I believe that in the beginning we also were light. the star lit sky
was breathed into existence by a fire breathing God, he controls
the elements and where they occur.

<u>Luggage</u>

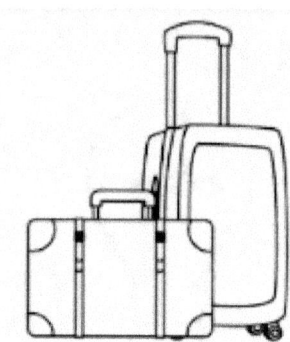

The damage done, the hearts not won, swimming in despair.
You've made your choice, you raised your voice how could you even dare.
I tried my best with little rest to change your life for the good,
but you lost my trust, do what you must and I'll just knock on wood.
You think you can guilt me for the past that will never do, the problem I see isn't with me the problem is with only you.
I wrote this as a reaction to a tantrum my 18-year-old daughter threw

Quantum

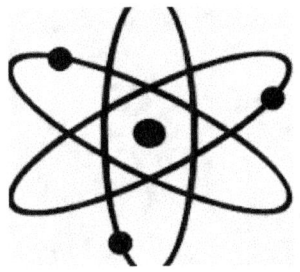

I sit here in my train of thought, thumbing through the days of
not, weary from the thought's I should not think.
In my troubled anxious mind, the peace I fear I cannot find in
dangerous waters I begin to sink. Was it for a promise made?
in all the years I sat delayed afraid to walk as I could hardly
breath. I summon all my inner strength a difficult chore of
chaotic length, to overcome the fear inside of me.
Now I drift along the tide believing that place where I abide,
can walk another mile in my shoes. In a far and distant land the
laws on which we now do stand, are just the poison thorns that
come in twos. My intent is not to be understood as I've done the
very best I could to see the day that I might understand you.
I did not come to help you up, to drink your wine from a silver
cup for that my dear would only make me blue.
just my thoughts on a lazy Saturday, just the parts in my mind
written on paper so to speak

<u>Water fall</u>

The actions of a desperate soul burning long and out of control
should never pass the boundaries set in me.
As wisdom escapes me I cannot feel the feelings in you so
unreal are lost when they are drowning in the sea.
Something that you might say in a break-up.

<u>Let It Go</u>

What will we gain behind a door full of hate? surrounded by
what we abhor.
For all the resentments we clutch in our fist, for hatred we all
scream for more.
What can we do with this strong aversion? we scratch and we
pick at the sore, just let it go, when we reap what we sew my
friends simply close tight the door.

<u>The Lynching</u>

I watched as the white men's whipped the boy so hard and so many times that those small bones on his spine became visible under all that blood.

His momma cried out, please!!! be merciful, and it was her blood curtailing cry that made them stop.

She had four of her neighbors cut his lifeless body down from the rope they tied around his small little hands, she knew she would bury him the very next day.

A man cannot be judged by the color of his skin, tell that to a man that has hatred bred into him the moment he learned to speak.

The moment he learned why he was different because of the color of his skin.

I totally detest racism, all men and all women are my brothers and my sisters

<u>Freedom reigns</u>

I have a need to express my feeling on how I no longer feel free. The masks that we wear to keep us from sickness are the sickness to me.

The driver of our weekly shuttle always makes us wear two. To me it's just another pain in the ass, I have to ask friends how about you?

I believe we're on a path to something so scary in silence I pick at the sore.

In darkness I find the enemy unkind tells me we're headed to war.

I will keep praying, ill hope for the best but I believe that we all know the score.

For I've the freedom at heart, it's a good place to start I don't need anything more.

Anybody's Guess

Hurriedly we shuffle in and out of black, we dig and dig looking to find all the things we lack. Are we made of memories? of a better past? will we come to know the truth? good things never last. So profound and lucid are the men of No, they'll chew you up then spit you out for all things come, then go.
Someday we'll take a trip to Yes and find that thing we need, or we can cut a broken heart just to watch it bleed.
I traveled to the land of We but not one soul was found, then I came to a place called Scream and did not hear a sound.
This may all but confuse you, a cheap old parlor trick, I can also bring the light on a candle absent wick.
For I am a believer in that which we cannot see, a traveler lost in distant lands invisible to me. These words are just semantics, meant to entertain, I will never pick your nose but I will pick your brain.

<u>My Companion</u>

With you I tread softly, I watch what I say, it's out of respect
that I treat you this way.

The journey has come down to one simple thing, to keep
pushing forward to the fruit it may bring. Hinds feet in high
places for the cliffs we must climb, we better get at it before we
run out of time. You see one strand of rope is weaker than two,
I am much stronger when I travel with you. Sometimes you
might doubt me but be of good cheer, for there is a legion of
angels standing guard for us here.

Their eyes are like fire, and their swords are ablaze, and they
will protect us as we enter the maze. All manner of creatures
will be on our path, if danger surrounds us we will sit down
and laugh. I've my bow and some arrows to eat what we kill,
the road it gets narrow, the other side of this hill. When this is
over and it comes to the end, ill thank God in heaven that you
were my friend

Hmmmmmmm...

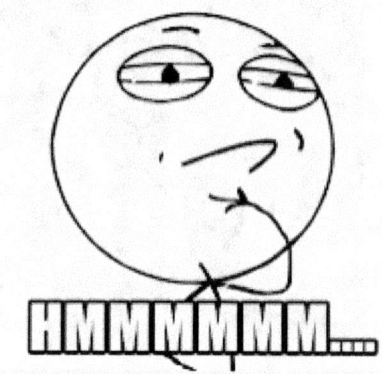

For those who are the people that we think that we can trust, are more than just the faces looking back at us. We are creatures of habit and the bad ones look to do us in, Knowing the good we should do and not doing it is the greatest sin.

Where will my neighbor go? to get the help he needs, I don't claim to know the answer I'm just here to plant the seeds.

With a world full of ego's some are swimming in vanity. Stay on path don't forget to laugh and keep your sanity. Don't be afraid to spread the love don't let your heart be filled with hate, do it now because tomorrow? it may be too late.

<u>My King</u>

Birds are singing, flowers full blossom, love is in the air. We travel down our happy road without one single care. Here there is no drama, our banner clothed in peace, the troubles are few, our hearts are brand new our eye's fixed on the east. Someday soon he's going to come this second time around, keep the faith saved by his grace, you were lost but now your found. Life is all around us, it is in the air we breathe, stay in the light and fight man fight! for the things you really need. For all of those that read this poem, my motives are good and clean. My symbol is love and a pure white dove with Jesus as my king.

<u>My Life Shall Remain</u>

I shall live every moment as though it were my last, my faith
mixed with courage will not allow my wall's to be breached.
As if a raging storm! should threaten all that I hold dear, my
'will' remains strong as now I know and believe my soul is
eternal and my spirit the same.
Nothing could separate me from life with a promise. My cup is
full and so my life shall remain.

A Better Life

What was I in the old life? A beggar and a thief. Anything just
to try and fill the hole inside of me. Sometimes I drank so much
whiskey, my face was on the floor, it didn't really matter to me I
always cried for more.
Then began the drug use, my dilated eye's, I lost it all as I began
fall created my demise.
My poor family were disgusted from the choices that I made.
My judgement blurred and my hope deferred because I couldn't
make the grade.
This is not self-pity, it's just the way I rolled, the angels had my
spirit, but the devil had my soul. I've put that life behind me,
I live for better days, I have got my blessing, but Jesus gets my
praise.

<u>Only You</u>

I see you through the looking glass, your eye's a vibrant blue.
Your hair so long and black drawls me in to your waiting arms.
I'm so grateful for the love you share tis my pleasure to give
it back in a passionate moment and to feel my body entangled
with yours breathing full, the scent of your blossom like a wines
bouquet turns me into a heated lion which fiercely takes its
prize.
You alone are the woman I dream of, knowing, feeling, holding
and loving only you.

My Take on Heaven

My mind is a kingdom where hunger and pain do not reside.
It's a place with golden harmonies and there is no need to hide.
Here there are no beggars because everyone is fed.
The gardens grow every kind of fruit and here the weeds are
dead. No one here gets offended, no insults will you hear. now
there's only courage, say goodbye to all you fear.
Everyone has a neighbor, no one is alone, you can come and go
just as you please every doggy has a bone.
There are every kind of creatures and they come and go in
two's, you can run a race with a cheetah, but you are gonna
lose. These things that are aforementioned will fill your heart
with peace, this is how it's going to be as he's ascending in the
east. This is an idea of heaven and how it just might be, this gift
cannot be earned you see? because this gift is free.

<u>My Riddle</u>

Thoughts moving in and through the flux of time. Numerical odyssey, an endless highway of formulas and nexus with ideals meant to entertain do all they can to baffle this brain that uses a small percentage of the minds total realm, thus granting me a key to an endless mansion full of all the answers I'll ever need but never telling me why.

You can put a round peg in a square hole, 2x2=4 pi squared will reveal the diagonal distance between two points on a two inch offset.

The point is, we are everyone of us intelligent truth seekers on the verge of great inventions that will no doubt be of great use to humanity. Here's hoping.

<u>Real Victory</u>

Do you feel the hope all around you? is it something you can touch? or is it something that confounds you? or does it matter much? I know what it feels like to be forgotten, lost and drunk from shame, my heart decayed and rotten, drenched in hate and blame.

You are not alone my friend I've been there before, locked in my own prison, in four walls without a door.

Even now the past doe's haunt me and tricks me to believe, that I am still a prisoner wearing my feelings on my sleeve. It's then that I remember that I have been set free, the past that I surrender has lost its hold on me. To you I say' keep on fighting! for someday you will win, and the story you'll be telling is that it didn't do you in.

The Reason That I Glow

I write the poem before the title it humbly speaks to me. My brains on go it's rarely idle the right words I do seek. You see, I need a buffer as I don't want to do you harm.

I am you and then another as your reaction keeps me warm. There are some words that I consider are just not right for me.

I am forgiving never bitter only because my heart is free. I learned a great deal by reading the awesome poems you wrote. And I long to hear a greeting as it keeps my ship afloat. All of you are my mentors, you teach me what I need to know. You are intelligent poem inventors, the reason that I glow.

<u>Pulse</u>

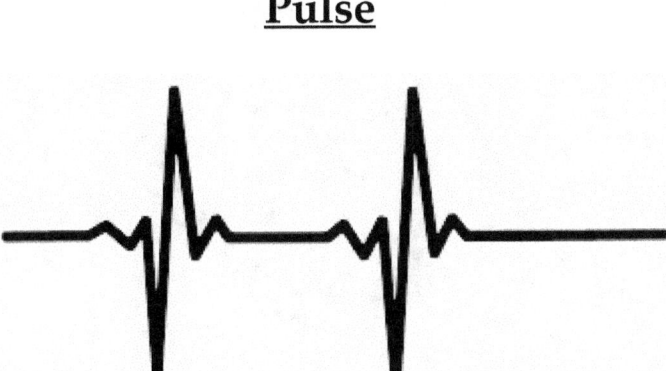

Lights on low my heart beats in a melodic contour, lightly I feel
each pulse.
Gone are the aspirations of bygones that seamlessly drip
through the cracks ever reminding me of the flux in time is an
ironic proclamation for time does not move back and forth, time
constantly moves ahead.

<u>My Endeavor</u>

At first I raised some questions, like what's the deal with him?
with a flashlight strapped around my head and my mustache
kind of thin. It's ok you see I get it when we meet somebody
new, we are skeptical and careful and a little judgmental too.
There are some tool's that I picked up that I found along the
way, patients are my favorite one, then watching what I say.
For the days that I am angry then I just take a break. To think on
things that calm me down, why not! for heaven's sake.
When it comes to giving, at that I am a king, to be kind and go
on living, in my heart a song to sing. I could go on forever on
this rollercoaster ride, love is my endeavor with an angel by my
side.

Early is the Hour

Early is the hour the moon is a shining hue; I can see the tower twenty feet ahead of you. Dark is this star filled sky, what a sight to see. A natural induced heavy nighttime high that takes ahold of me. Thunder speaks and lightning flashes one hell of a show.

It knocks us right down off our asses we keep the volume low. We make preparations for our journey and the dangers we might face, we keep the night fire high and burning nothing goes to waste.

Our ship is stout and it will protect us it's made of wood and steel, no diseases will infect us and all our wounds will heal. We will not cower for one minute, courage is our creed, I know the shit cause I've been in it fighting to be freed!

<u>These Things</u>

Children laughing, hands-a-clapping, music playing feet are
tapping. Sun is shining, rivers flowing, gardens tilled, veggies
growing. Anniversaries, rappers rapping, doggies in the
backyard crapping.
Big promotion, bigger paycheck, bought a sailboat, named it
bad-wreck.
Now we're living not just surviving, you can tell I'm rich by the
car I'm driving.
People taking dreams they're dreaming, babies in the carriage
screaming.
Just got married moved in to a big house, in the kitchen found a
dead mouse. Found some money then I spent it, tried renting a
car but couldn't rent it. the end. smiles.

The Key and The Door

Thoughts are dancing in my mind as venting blocks for me. I
listen as the speaker talks and says 'you need a key' this came to
behoove me as I aloud the words to speak.
It's crucial that I listen for the answers that I seek. He then then
brought forth a challenge, the key I had to find. Was always
there inside me in the corner of my mind.
What good is the key inside me if I cannot find the door? The
stark repudiation with my eye's fixed on the floor.
The speaker then surprised me a master at his art, the door you
seek is inside you on the right side of your heart.

A Poem from the Book of Psalms

My children do not forget my teaching, keep my commandments then you shall win favor and a good name in the eyes of God and man. let love and faithfulness never leave you. Bind them around your neck and write them on the tablet of your heart. In all of your way's acknowledge him and he will make your path straight.

The Band

Things are in motion, the rhythm steady and slow. The
drumbeat tells the others which way they need to go.
The man on the piano, his fingers spark up a flame, the
keyboard stepping to it because badass is her name. The vocals
are amazing the high notes sharp and clean, the bass is really
thumping, the very best that I've ever seen.
I can't forget the bongo's you can tell this guy's a pro, give this
man a solo then just sits and watch him go.
One thing they have in common is they play like they are one,
they will all but blow your mind before the night is done.

The One You Feed the Most

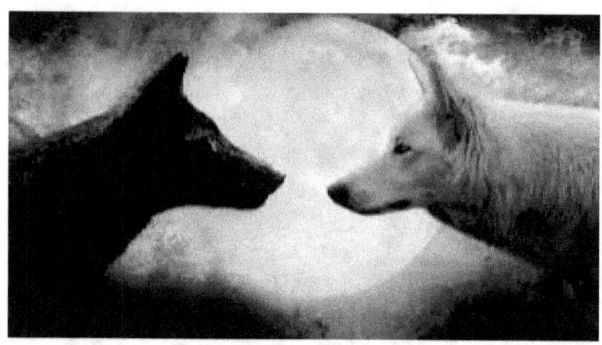

The break of day, the dawning night, shadows creeping,
avoiding light. Sharp and long his fangs and teeth, the wolf is
craving blood and meat. Beware of his presence, run and hide, it
may mean your peril if your paths collide.
Heed this warning while you're on your way, you won't be safe
until night turns to day.
I am apologetic for this crass charade, if I don't tell it right then
I'll never get paid. As for this wolf there are actually two, you'll
find both of them dwelling deep within you.
Now for the good wolf he's forgiving and kind, He will bring
you to safety and never leave you behind.
When your sad or in pain he will sit by your side, when you
need a friend then you won't be denied, his anger is righteous
in a flash it is gone, feed the good wolf for the journey you're on.

The Rest

The day has ended I had a blast looking toward the future forgetting the past. Relinquishing thoughts designed to bring guilt, the idea that I'm unworthy is starting to wilt. None of us are perfect we know this cliché, but I stand a pillar at the end of the day. My soul waits in heaven and when my time here is through, my spirit will join him there's so much to do. There will be celebrations with Jesus our king, we'll gather with angels and we'll stand-up and sing. No negative thoughts will enter our hearts, if someone is hurting it shall end as it starts. So while you are here let your life be the best, don't live in anger and you know the rest.

Every Minute Past Three

Her piercing eye's looked straight through my soul, her mouth
opened wide could swallow me whole. She practiced white
magic, a detestable sin, she opened her door and invited me in.
Once I was inside she chanted a spell, she summoned a demon!
right out of hell.
She claimed she had powers beyond all beliefs, saying, she
could move mountains as she prayed to the east. Just then I
was moved by the God that I serve, she knew something was
different and started losing her nerve.
I said 'what will become you when it's your turn to die? will all
this be worth it when your name is denied? I told her' in heaven
there's a book full of names, I said ' you must be in it' to avoid
all the flame's.
She thought for a minute her eye's fixed on the floor she gave
me her answer as she opened her door. She claimed Satan was
her god with the demon she raised, she said hell was Europa
while she offered him praise. My friends there is a battle with
demons and more, do not be deceived, please! don't walk
through that door. Hell is a real place! in a realm we can't see,

and there you will suffer every minute passed three.

<u>The Day</u>

It's half past the hour it this morning time for me. I'm dwelling on the future and for what it holds to be. I do not want for anything as all my needs are met. The cards I hold I will not fold I gladly make a bet. Life is for the living we need lay the dead to rest. Unafraid I keep on giving because it just might be a test. The sun is out; the birds are singing there's a fragrance in the air. In the distance are church bells ringing notes are riding everywhere.

This small town life has its own rhythm all my neighbors say hello. A fine place to raise your children, to lay back and watch them grow.

Now? I'm back to the moment that is where I need to live. I at times run out of money just because I love to give.

I Dig for the Gold

When I am feeling low and ungrateful , just like life just isn't fair.

It is in these day›s that I am amazed thinking I really don't care. Emotions and our feelings lie to us, it's better to go by what we know, our thoughts also very dubious in poisoned soil where nothing can grow.

It is crucial that I raise my defenses when I am depressed feeling down. I stay aware of my seven senses wearing a smile instead of a frown.

It's never easy sometimes it's hard work, to be a man honest and true. I Dig for the gold and I value my soul. I have to ask friend how about you?

We Are What We Ate

What if we all stand? come together as one. Lay down the nuke's, put down the gun. What if we all started giving? to all those in need.

What if we listen? to those hurting and planted a seed. What if we cared for our planet? and did what is right. What if we gave someone hope? When their money was tight?

What if we befriended the lonely and gave them some faith? What if we respected our elders? then it would be great. What if we picked up the love? then put away all the hate. What if we finally realized? that we are what we ate.

It's Not You, It's Me

These words that I'm writing come straight from my heart, I write to amuse you is a good place to start. I write because I love it 'the highs and the lows' sometimes I blow it, that's just how it goes.
As for the topic I choose them with care, just like my clothes and the shoes that I wear.
I rarely get comments just the" love and the liked" it kinda hurts me but I'm doing alright.
These poems that I'm writing are priceless to me, the ones about doors, the occasional key.
I am constantly evolving and I'm opened for change, I strive to be better but it's out of my range. I wrote this poem cause I want you to see, it doesn't really matter, it's not you it's me.

Another Day

Another day has revealed itself to me, the wonders of life never cease to amaze me.

Whatever You Do

whatever YOU ARE be a GOOD ONE

Dear reader; I'm writing to tell you that I am brimming with hope, I know I won't find the answer at the end of a thick knotted rope. I thought of my loved one's and the pain they would feel, and the wounds cutting deep and never to heal. I know there's an answer to the problems I face, I know I will find it if I lean on God's grace. I also believe that I might need a hand, someone with insight who might understand. As my trouble is with me, I know it shall pass, then I shall sing praises as I lift up my glass. I'm here to tell you that I wrote this for you, so please just hang in there whatever you do. My friend you are precious beyond what you know, never check out before it's your time to go.

My Soulmate

Even though we're miles apart, I still feel your presents in the pit of my heart. Your big brown eyes, the feel of your stare, the way that that you listen and tell me you care. Running my finger's down the nape of your back, the way that you love me despite the things that I lack. The scent of your fragrance, the perfume just a bit, the fire that's burning is the one that you lit. We love from a distance though your far away, we're still together at the end of the day. Our love is eternal and will always be, you are my soul-mate the one that God gave to me.

The Memoirs of a Junkie

These are the Memoirs of a junkie, torn between addiction and pain, this is his unholy affliction when he's dope sick it drives him insane. Twenty-four seven he's hurting, the withdrawals are so hard to bare, with no one to help him he's searching, for hours he just sits and stares. Now the cold sweats and the vomit, two days since he had his last fix, he finds a bag of dope in his coat pocket and fills his rig with one point two six. For now, he isn't sweating or hurting but he knows that his high will not last, he lays his head down and drawls the curtain and dreams of a good dope free past. This was my life the way I lived it, my addiction laid hold on my soul, I had a damn and I gave it! now I'm clean and I'm becoming whole

<u>Eternal</u>

Our lives will be over all things come to pass, so live yours
to the fullest and your memory will last. Dwell on the hard
times with the lessons you learned, you danced in the fire and
you didn't get burned. One day at a time is all that we get, be
patient and kind, not bottled up with regret. We are getting
closer all journeys come to an end, be forever grateful if you had
one good friend. As we die we pass from this life to the next, if
we get separated simply send me a text. We will bask in glory
and sing praises out loud, we will be able to fly and sit on the
clouds. There we will be eternal never again will we die; we
shall meet the king before our very eyes. For ever eternal a new
life to live, forever eternal, a new life to live.

<u>Cut Short</u>

Their love
though unhurried
left something of a bitter taste
upon both the palette and the tongue …

…

Yes indeed,
it seemed, their love
was exhausted long before
their journey together had officially begun …

<u>If Truth Was a Colour</u>

If truth was a colour
It would not be green

…

Green is for forests
And gardens and envy

…

If truth was a colour
It would have to be blue …

Sheen

Somewhere behind these eyes
the seed of a soul does barely hide ..

...

A kaleidoscope within a rainbow
prismed ..
Like petrol on still water, glistens ..

...

The sheen
upon a starling's back imprisoned ..

...

A stolen kiss,
a glimpse, an elliptical eclipse ..

...

A fleeting iridescent glint, and presence
no longer felt, yet still smiling, albeit blindly ..

Childhood

Humpty Dumpty, the big bad wolf, the old woman whom lived in a shoe, Tinkerbell and Peter Pan the stories we once knew. When I was a child my innocence and the tales my mother told, the warmth I feel is still so real even though I'm growing old. Pillow fights and hide and go seek with four square at the park, playing games, making cool air-planes and flying them in the dark. These are reminders of childhood day's when I was still care free, the thrill I knew within me grew the things that I could see. These are my childhood memories that take my breathe away, my treasures of a distant past are with me still today.

I Assume Someone Does

warmth, cascades mingling with invisible sky currents. Black holes with what lies deep within, a star falls victim to its gravitational pull, sending it to parts unknown to man. The mathematical theories arrive endlessly as we geologically make futile attempts to map our hugely unknown universe. It is an ideal worthy of investigations and summary, who knows ' I assume someone doe's yeah? you tell me.

An Old Dusty Self

This goes out to those hurting, drowning in sorrow and shame. To those that don't feel at all worthy, listen I'll try to explain. You are more than what you see in a mirror, much more than your bone and your skin, your soul and your spirit eternal, valued high above this world that we're in. We in our arsenal have mercy, love and respect in there too, you have loved ones that can't live without you, am I just now getting through? It's time that you did some forgiving, starting first with yourself, now is the time to start living, not stuck on an old dusty shelf. My friend though I've never met you, we are brothers and sisters for real, I could never forget you, in time old battle wounds will be healed. Your life is precious, your wanted, I am not too far away, I'll pray for you every night my friend, then I'll pray every day.

Early Morning Thursday

Early morning Thursday reveal yourself to me, I know that you gave me fare warning, slowly you snuck up about three. I wait with great expectations, I wait to see what you will bring, synchronized evaluations, a beautiful song will you sing. Early morning Thursday I love you, deep within the depths of my soul, we'll sing a song but you hit the high notes, your beautiful voice never gets old. Early morning Thursday we're just being, there is nothing else I'd rather do, the lights emanating I'm seeing, shine on me and then? back on you.

<u>Of All Things</u>

Black man, brown man, native man, white! who will be my bro. tonight? all men, any men slave or free who will be a friend to me?

Muscle man, weak man, short man, tall. I will give respect to all.

<u>Journey</u>

Where can I go? for the answers I seek, I've walked for miles
with my legs getting weak. Is there a wise man? whom might
know the way, I won't need it tomorrow, I need it today.
Where are the scholars? where have they gone? Lord give
me strength for this journey I'm on. I've been alone with no
comfort, no peace, still I keep walking my eye's fixed to the
east. Long is this journey with no end in sight, I pray not for
darkness, I pray for the light.
I'll keep on going I have to be strong, I am so tired but I must
carry on. Soon I'll be sleeping and I hope that I dream, I can hear
the water of a slow moving stream.
A still quiet voice is guiding my way, so I'll keep on going
through my mind wants to stay. I've come to a clearing, I hear a
song, I've come to the end of this journey is done.

I

I feel his power every day, I see his light and it's here to stay I
see you through eyes of love and with grace. There is one Jesus
and I've seen his face. I have been admonished when I was
wrong, his anger is here and then it is gone.
I have seen mercy while others have not, I have been threatened
and then I have fought. I've seen a beggar and brought him
some food, I've seen disrespect from a child so rude.
I have seen someone lost and showed them the way, I have
been tired at the end of the day.
I've seen forgiveness, a wonderful thing, I've seen the sparrow
and I've heard it sing. These are my treasures which I hold true,
just one more thing that I see in you.

<u>Supernova</u>

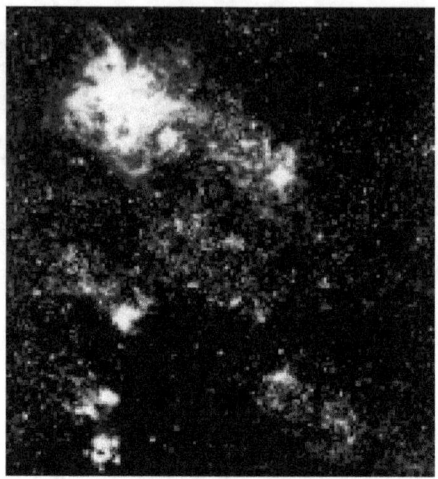

He breathed life into stars and constellations, a celestial sphere
gives a home to stars that speak.
Our universe, full of all things spoken into existence and so they
do.

That Day

Somewhere along the way a thought was planted on that day, keep searching and the truth you'll find, your memory of the life unkind, a feeling and it drove you mad, there is no time for feeling sad. You pictured a much better past, I'm sorry that you came in last.

You kept on running from what you need the most like Jesus giving up the ghost.

You dwell on a dream that spoke, your words could make the children choke. Swinging on a barbed wire fence, spilling hatred for the mind so dense.

A pillow on which to lay your head is nothing for the dream that's dead.

You are lost and can't find your way, hated for the games you play. In terror you stop to look around, trying to run but can't find the ground. If this really speaks to you, you're not alone for I hear it to. A soft spoken word that kills, dirty rags for the blood that spills. Somewhere along the way a thought was planted on that day.

Paradigm

We are in a paradigm, words spoken in declension tarring away the fabric of good morals and worthy values. Children not respecting their parents, immoralities and sexual perversion as all interests are now the accepted norm. Where do we go from here?

<u>Sad</u>

I pray for the lonely, I know how you feel. Dusty floors and
broken doors, a heart that never heals. Unspoken words of
apathy, the lies they feed your mind, you have no friends is how
it ends they treat you so unkind. Within your darkness takes
ahold, squeezing tight around your soul. anarchy in the air we
breathe, should you stay or should you leave?
No one will come to your aid, the sun is out you have no shade,
drenched in total disregard, the reason that your heart is hard,
slowly compass find a star, no one knows just where you are.
Slowly hurt you don't know why, now it's time for you to die.

A Way

Like a ghost I walk the landscape searching for a way, because the way I have right now is leaving me today. The way I have is all worn out, you can tell that it's been used, it's near the end and has no friend, it's heart is cut and bruised. May I find another way to walk inside my shoes, death is here it's getting near, the troubles come in two's. I've seen a man and I liked his way, he seemed happy all the time, I have a knife, I can take his life and leave my way behind. I'm no killer I'll let him go and he can have his way, my way is used but it's paid its dues, I guess it's here to stay.

<u>God's Will</u>

I lit the tinder, I created the fire, I humbly accepted the title of
Sire.
I ruled my people with grace and forgiveness, then they were
judged with fire and fairness, no one there hungered, all had a
home there. On Sunday we gathered together in deep prayer.
If we were in battle and somebody died brave, we honored his
widow and respected the life gave.
We worshiped in truth and then in spirit, when the priest gave
a message all there could hear it. This is an idea of a strong
healthy kingdom, where all walks of life are all more than
welcome.

Change Everything

I'm making some changes inside and out, I like what I'm seeing
without one single doubt.
First it started with my heart then my spirit and soul, I had to go
through it if I want to be whole.
I don't cut any corners with this path that I'm on, it hasn't been
easy and the journey's been long. I've learned to be patient, I
watch what I say, I study my actions at the end of each day.
I try to remember each promise I make; I've learned how to give
much more than I take.
I don't lust after women, I give them respect, I work to amend
every life I have wrecked. I no longer hold grudges, a big waste
of time, I no longer fight or commit any crime.
This is part of my story and I'm doing well, I no longer believe
that I'm going to hell. I've made peace with my maker and in
the end? he is my savior, my very best friend.

No More

Telling my story is so hard to do, the pain is so hard to bare, there is much I confess was a terrible mess, to what of it can I compare? there is so much you see?

So unsettled in me I would look out my window and stare. I had my first drink at age seven, I smoked my first bong hit at nine, at age fourteen I overdosed on tequila, I drank so much that I nearly died. From there my life seemed so confusing, I hardly knew what to do with my time, so I just kept on using to forget about this life of mine.

I lost every job that they gave me, I drank until I was a corpse, once I even went to Las Vegas and bet on a high loosing horse. In the eighties things just got harder as I got addicted to meth, my skin literally crawled as I stood by the wall and I prayed for a slow painful death. Now I've put it behind me, now I'm finally clean, it's been three years in the making with no more of that life for me.

<u>My World</u>

In the deepest, darkest of night you have invaded my dream.
Your ruby lips are full , beautiful pillows that when kissed by
them I am set on fire.
You must know that in that heat, that one simple act my blood
boils over consumed by your juices forcing me to swallow every
drop.
No other woman could take your place for you have branded
my ass with your name and I will always be ready to make
sweet, hard love with no interruptions, for I long to inhale every
part of you , my lover, my mate, my world.

Better Than

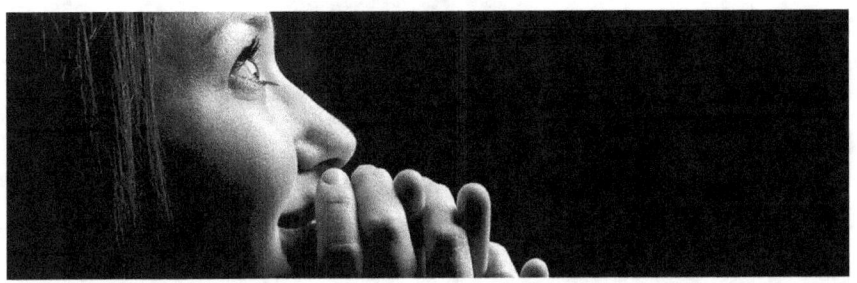

Better a small hut with peace and quiet than a
mansion full of feasting and selfish gain for too much of that
will drive you insane.

Better to live alone than to be with the one that you despise, you
can see her contempt in her hideous eye's.
Better to be poor and debt free than to have it all without peace
of mind.
Better to give and receive for to go without one or the other is
not wise.
Better to forgive than to harbor a grudge why die before your
time
Better to love than to hate for hatred is like poison which will
destroy a righteous man .
Better to die than to be born for birth is the beginning of woe's.

My Own Way

There will be a time
when we must choose
between what is easy,
and what is Right.
—A. DUMBLEDORE

No man has ever had knowledge of you, your virginity is a
well-kept secret.
Many men have pursued you only to find they were not worthy
of your treasure.
I have only gazed upon your beauty from afar, In the night I
dreamed an unholy dream, that one day I would ask for your
hand in righteous matrimony.
For you I will move mountains, I will cross the oceans to find
a vow I made in the dew drop morning, singing a song of true
love for I must tell you that in the dead of night I caressed
myself while thinking of you, please forgive my boldness as I
was without control.
But now I resign myself to give way to a suiter much younger
and more handsome than I, quietly, I go my own way.

<u>Only You</u>

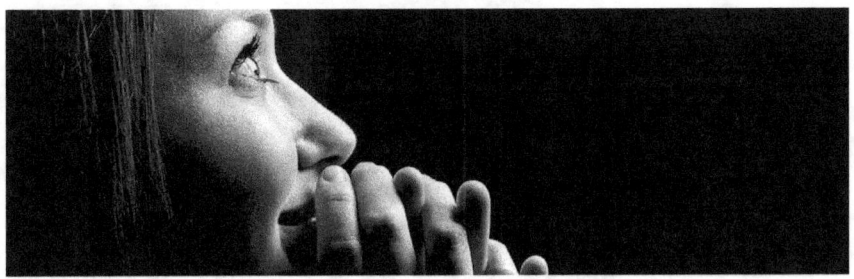

I dream in earnest about the curves of your frame, tantalizing
is the scent of your well. your hair is long and is like an ocean
wave that beckons my promise, you will never be nor should
you ever be tamed.

as you are young, you are wild and you are free
to be the woman you desire to be. It's your free will that draws
me in as many a men have tried but failed to see your mind,
your heart and your soul. that is my wealth, my passion and my
birth right to love only you.

<u>For You</u>

You are my sunshine!

Do you feel like your drifting? like doves gliding on the breeze? You feel so high as your kissing the sky and it brings you down to your knees.

Here there is nothing to be afraid of, here the lion lays with the lambs, how much love and respect do I dish out? 7.70 x70 grams.

For you see I love without limits, I 've learned to forgive every wrong, in our hearts we can be without hatred, we can all just get along.

In this world we will have trials, in this world we will know pain, love each person as we want to be loved again, again, and again. I am going to do my part as my higher power shows me to do, when it's all said and done both the work and the fun I'll be waiting in heaven for you.

Masks

Drowning in sorrow, I walk with a cane, it's real complicated
but I'll try to explain. When I was a child, the masks that were
worn were there to protect me since the day I was born.
I had a mother and a father you see, but that didn't stop the
beatings on me. I had nobody, I had not one friend, in school I
was bullied and harassed without end.
I prayed to Jesus but he never came, my teachers ignored me
they added to my shame. This is my story. I tell it with care,
why did this happen? why is life so unfair?
There are other children whom have it harder than me, they
hope for redemption, and a chance to be free.
Now I am older, and so blessed to be, now I have friends who
share their love and it's free, no more beatings but I still wear a
mask, I'll take it off if politely you ask.

<u>Dying Wish</u>

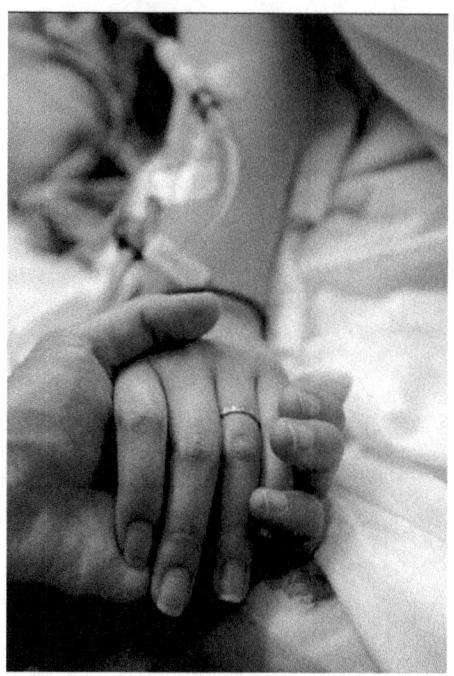

Sunlight glistening waves crashing down, living waters, you shall thirst no more. Inner beauty without blemish unflawed. Love unrequited is thigh reward.

A beating heart living long in your disdain, yours is a tumultuous companion, seek thee a dry quiet plain and there find your peace, not undone but complete without end for without it we are destined to die and whom will come?

No my friend, this will not be your story, you will sprout wings of an angel then? Just fly.

<u>Done</u>

In your hollow eyes is the story I seek, I may write in a day, or it might take a week. I'll start with the way you snatched all that I owned, my heart, my soul, my skin and my bone, you then took my feelings, you trampled them good the damage so hard to repair.

I sat in our room with a heart full of gloom, the sign on our wall read beware.

Who could I turn to? what could I do? as I sat on the porch and I wept. I had no friends that's the way that it ends.

I only had peace when I slept. I made up my mind I would never again get with a woman like you, you make my skin itch, you're a low bottom bitch, I'm thankful we're finally through.

Those Shoes

To many times did I trust you every chance that I gave you
bereaved , for hours I stood in the pouring rain with my feelings
all over my sleeve .
You were cold blooded and evil , what you did in secret was
known, your cheating way, at the end of the day was the only
thing that you owned .
Your smile was just a distraction, your well to do mask just a
ploy, the game that you played, smoking meth in the shade
robbed me of all of my joy.
I was the hopeless shell of a man, desperate and infested with
hate, while you popped pills with your friend, I was right near
the end, sitting outside by the gate.
Now the table is turned, now I am so rid of you, your weak little
mind is not much of a find, no longer do I walk in those shoes

So Thankful

I stand in front of a big white page I stand alone but I'm not forgotten, those that remember the days of old the memories are decayed and rotten.

Me? I'm older and the lessons. I've learned are riding upon my shoulders, the fire I breath, the lies that I weave warm me as the nights here grow colder.

I'm not a robot nor am I a machine I can feel every insult you throw me; you see? I am free it's the best way to be, if you think I am wrong, simply show me.

For paragraph 2 there is so much to do, I may need someone

to help me, no one shallow nor plain there is so much to gain
and you stretched out your hand then you felt me.

Here we reside with our flaws we denied because the truth
is always so painful, the lie I confess in this terrible mess is
forgotten and I am so thankful.

Goodnight

In my mind are wonders that the eye can't see, a wide array
of fractals that dwell inside of me. Mountain tops and plush
green valley's rule the opened plains, countless flowers are
everywhere I washed out all the stains.
Here you won't find negative thoughts but you will need a key,
I cannot let just anyone in that may be a threat to me.
Fluffy pillows and clean white sheets when it's time for bed,
puppy dog pets and no regrets are swimming in my head.
Here it's always summer but first it's always spring, wonderful
sounds echo through the air you can hear the angels sing, no
bad dreams nor nightmares only what's good and right, until
we meet again my friends I bid you all good night.

<u>Mental</u>

So here we are in the middle of winter I hunger for the spring, I
take 60 mgs of Adderall, grab my guitar and I sing.
For depression I take 40 mgs of Prozac to keep me off the edge,
suicide is not an option, get that right through my head.
I am a master of mental disorders bi polar through and through,
it's just a fact but I am not wacked I'm just telling you the truth.
I never get angry nor justify my actions when I know I am
wrong, let's live in peace and harmony why can't we just get
along?

Only a Test

The tiles are missing from the kitchen floor and there are no pellets for the stove, there is no heat nor warmth to cover me, no blankets did she wove.
Time just smiles and mocks my pain, it really could care less, nothing to do but count the beats deep inside my chest. Are there no visitors? Who will come? Does anybody care?
I mark the notches on my wall with a cold unloving stare.
Now it's time, make a choice, if I really want to be free, what is needed deep down below is a lock without a key.
This is the thing all good poets simply need to know, is how to move and manipulate words in every single row. This is it, the very last sentence, I hope you all the best.
I'm cutting the line, with no fish to find, it's only been a test.

Just a Thought

I search high and low, looking for truth in the innermost parts, my mind is a spiral stair case. Where I file my thoughts and store all of my dreams.

High and mighty in my mind I am king, searching for solace in a vast network of pods, nooks, and crannies.

In my travels I meet attitudes seemingly, without any emotion, perched above the latitude are vertical dwellings unfit for occupation, so they to this day are just empty shells waiting to be invaded.

Stop! for the road ahead has been washed away, forcing all to find another way back home.

<u>Unevolving</u>

I sit in my post-apocalyptic waste land pondering the ways of the world, a baby stroller blocks the entrance to a once inhabited night club, no more are there the sounds of people celebrating what at one time was life.

Degradation, Oprah Winfrey, Helen DeGeneres memories of better days, now there is famine, children are eating the ashes from old bomb debris, ladders only go down never up, welcome to the age of nuclear fallout, it's called that because it does make your hair fall out.

An alien is running the show claiming to be God but!!! he is an imposter handing out animal balloons.

Nobody is actually breathing as they are half dead half alive creatures of the night, smoking meth, drinking bathtub gin, grumbling and complaining because there just, isn't, anything else to do. farewell my friends it's been, interesting, ciao.

Perfect Peace

I stand alone against an army, I stand in line my turn to die, I muster all my faith and courage without ever asking why. There are many in the valley, there they wait to decide, they don't know that they are warriors, in God's power they do abide.
In the clouds God's mighty army, that are with the one afraid, I can count at least one legion, many ran but one man stayed.
It's never too late to be forgiven for the prince of peace is here, just say a simple prayer to Jesus he is always standing near.
Lord forgive me my heart is heavy, all weighed down with sin and grief, I lay my all at your feet Lord, all my sins for perfect peace.

Life? or death?

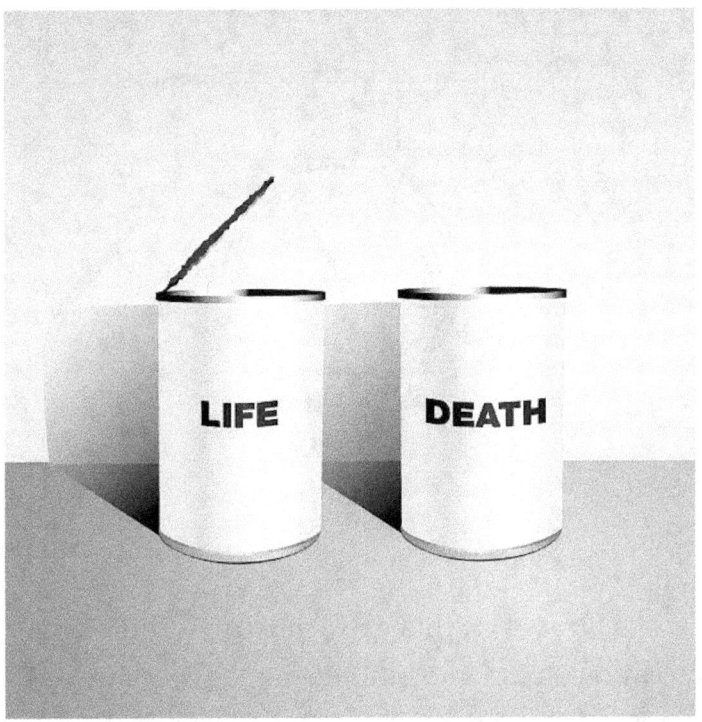

How can truth be shared in this apocalyptic waste land? and why are the masses so offended by it? it all comes down to what we see, and what we feel.

I am living proof that a being far greater than I molded and shaped me, at times he chipped away useless fragments that did me no earthly good and still what this being adds is far better than what he removes.

My friends the tree of life is far healthier than the tree of knowledge, In the end the choice is yours. Life? or death?

In Time

As I travel on this path, narrow is the way.
My companion's pain and suffering, the woes are here to stay.
They are not to be compared with the glory which lay ahead, for
there I'll bask in perfect peace with a crown upon my head.
To all of you I say take your place in heaven up above, there we
will walk on streets of gold cast into his perfect love.
This is what I need to know when fear and doubt creep in, he
gave his life upon that cross, I gave him my sin. So if you find
your running low I know how you feel, take it easy as you go in
time your wounds will heal.

<u>COVID from China to US</u>

The tide is slowly rising, death is in the air, traffic comes to an overly crowded highway now a congested and endless mess. Who is my enemy? What does he hope to gain as the platform twists and turns to an unwanted guest?

I'm going down into the depths. I'm going to murder anyone that stands in my way, evil man beware because you don't want to be on the receiving end of my wrath, because of you we're chocking and spewing out the toxic air you brought upon this our free soil and it shall forever remain free of your communist intent.

When the shit hits the fan I wouldn't want to be you. This is our sacred ground, tread softly for you tread on my values, my desires and my dreams, these will be the boundaries we set for you as we march you back to the rock you crawled out from.

We shall never conform to your ways; this is my putting you on notice! deal with it bitch

<u>Bring Hell to an End</u>

Dear God, I approach you as a humble friend, I ask you to please bring hell to an end, the thief's the liars the suicides, please let them with you abide.

Lord forgive me I ask so much, have mercy on those whom suffer such.

I am certain they've learned their lesson there bring hell to an end it's only fair, there must be something you can do, nothing is too big for you.

Lord, I beg thee this poem I send, Lord please bring hell to an end.

Lord everyone there knows the score, shut it down and bolt the door. I have to ask you once again, Lord please!! bring hell to an end.

<u>YOU</u>

You are my sunshine!

You must know that your special. there is no other like
you, your giving and kind, your one heck of a find no other
description will do.
I've watched you very carefully, sometimes you give till it hurts.
You worry and fret and you count your regrets and wonder if
you have any worth.
I am here to tell you your value is more precious than gold, and
the lies you believed as you were being deceived are dying,
crippled and old.
It's time to put down the hammer, your heart is beat up black
and blue, it's time to heal as you learn how to feel, you see I
need to learn these things too.

<u>My Point of View</u>

Long and wide is the road to hell, many there be that find it.
The devil promised them riches and fame, with a contract and
they up and signed it.
Some believe that hell is the world, their sorrows are many to be
counted, if you come across a bag full of woe's, leave that shit
where you found it.
I'm just a spectator leaving my mark in a world full of grave
confusion, the grass being greener on the other side of town is
just a grand illusion.
I'm certain of many things' that this life has taught me, when I
was falling, spiraling out of control Jesus reached out his hand
and he caught me. All of you have value and worth, if your
struggling my friend's just hang in there, I assume that you
know the rest, I believe life can be fair.

Walk On

Life is here but for only the living, are you trapped in the dark never giving? Are you down for the challenge that I'm bringing before you? In my heart I love and adore you.

Mesmerized by the way that I say it, if you're playing a game then go on and play it.
The merry-go-round that you ride around there, has to stop no one said life would be fair. I'm writing about what this ugly world up and gave me, not once did anyone offer to save me. It's not a resentment, I hold no grudges I'm not the stubborn mule that never budges.
Now I'm in the mix, I got that paper, I picked up the love and I put down the razor.
These days' I am loved, that is my treasure, this is my gift of significant measure.
The day's turn to night so I'll leave the light on, now you're a man and it is time to walk-on.

Breathe

I dread the day, wrapped around my neck the taker's come out
to play, stealing statues from their neighbor's yard's, they tell
you they bought them at Walmart.
Their lives are made up of routine's, they come and they go
never finding a quiet place to lay their heads.
I too at one time did follow a crowd of people that stole my self-
respect.

What will I gain by hating those that found amusement as I
coiled up like an infant going through with-drawls.
It's an uncertain life as I traded my soul for a drug that took
away my pain, be it for just a little while, that is all I wanted, it
was the only solace I could find.
Those that used me and loaded me with guilt as many-a-time I
tried to run away, but I had nowhere to go.
Today I am a free man, those that hurt me are in my rear view
mirror, now? I can breathe.

<u>Keep Your Feet Dry and Clean</u>

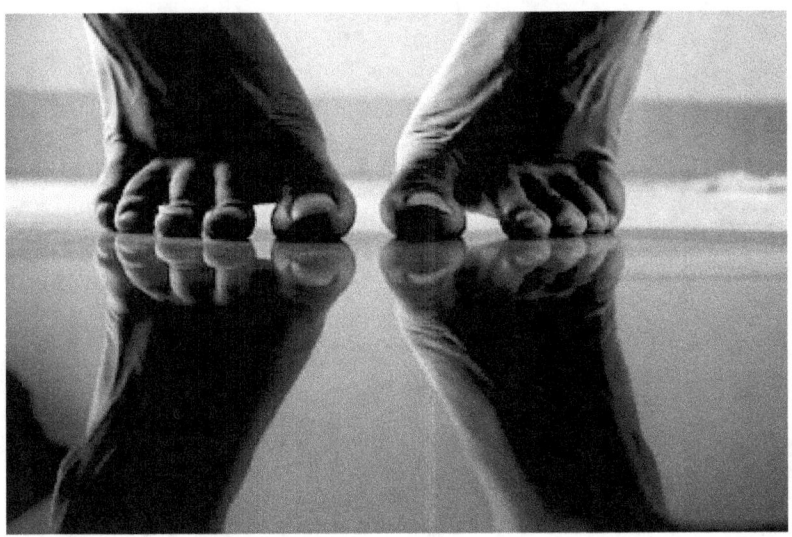

I've been in a funk and it's cramping my style someone please come feed the beast, on my neck he is breathing his anger is seething, he thought he would dine on a feast.

My mind is made up, I'm pissed off and fed up, if he move's just one more inch, I gave him fare warning, I'll be glad in the morning and be rid of his foul smelling stench.

In this life we have choices we just need use our voices and sometimes we might make a scene, do what you must, leave your foe's in the dust, in the end keep your feet dry and clean.

<u>Fight to Give</u>

We're like dog's in a corner itching to bite, when push comes to shove we are in for a fight.

This is the way I feel it needs to be, we have to throw punches if we want to be free.

When the fighting is over, it's time for peace, it's the way I prefer to say the least.

It's been said love thy neighbor as we want to be loved, my friend's we can do this with help from above.

Please know as you read this it's a good way to live, don't be a taker and learn how to give.

In all of my years I've come to believe, it's better to give than it is to receive.

I'll leave this impression and you can be the judge, how much should we give? what we have is enough.

Put Down Your Gun

I'm having a hard time, I'm failing to see, late is the hour for
you and for me.
As for what to write I've made a list, punching my pillow with
the ball of my fist.
I will be candid, I'll make it clear, not knowing what come's next
is the what' that I fear.
We all of us have value, all of us have worth, we all begin dying
at the time of our birth. Rhadamanthine, now there's a big
word, it mean's incorruptible and a chance to be heard.
So I will forge a new iron I will lead without fear, because I
know how to follow so be of good cheer. When it's all over, all
said and done, pick up the love and put down your gun.

<u>MY LIFE</u>

My life has been a long winding road, lonely and tired no
sympathy showed.
I hold to no grudges , no resentments nor hate , I've learned
some hard lessons the first? was to wait.
In this life of trials I seldom did know , the love of a father and
onward I go.
Still I'm no sceptic, it's plain to see? the scars on this heart
beating inside of me.
They are not random, I know every one, each has a name, the
damage is done.
Now I am older, wiser for the wear, I look to the future with a
thousand-yard stare. one more round for the end of the show,
the cuts come quickly but the healing is slow.

<u>Kneel</u>

The still morning slumber, the thousand-yard stare, the children
eat ashes but why should we care?
The mephitic bodies lye dead on the floor, ten to a pile we make
room for more.
Repine by nature, why shouldn't we be. we open our eye's still
we're to blind to see.
To the lost and those hurting that need to be heard, to offer
them healing and a couple kind words.
So kneel at the altar, acknowledge your shame, brother forgive
me and I'll do the same.

The Definition of Us

My mind is a spiral stair case and there you just might see , that
I am just like one of you , and you are just like me .
I've been told that I look angry , the dent between my eyes , it
came from years of public abuse and cut me down to size.
Still I just keep trying and I will never quit, because the role of
this old soul is no stranger to the shit. If you have seen what I've
seen, to what can I compare?
P T S D for you and for me and the one hundred-thousand-yard
stare.
So, we shall keep on trying and we shall never quit, instead
we'll fly thru the clear blue skies and keep our candles lit.

<u>Free</u>

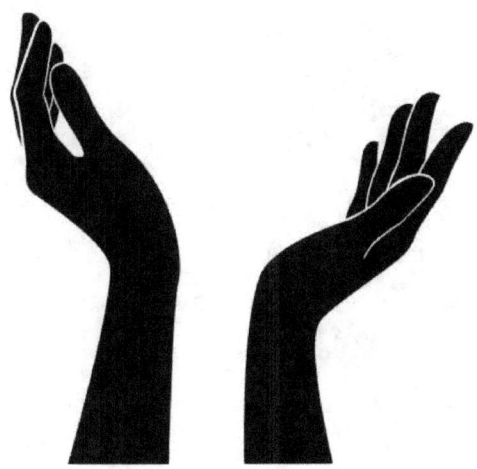

The jagged edge of a single thought will rip open the flesh,
unrelenting agony at the hands of a heart breaker.
I search my soul at the inner most parts, truth unfolds hardly
making a sound, lie's to pass the time, ugly is your deceit.
Your reward shall be utter torment for you would not suffer me
to weep as I lost all that I love. Oh my soul why are you down
cast?
You have never known the warmth of true love, you struggle as
a fish in a net.
When will I be shown mercy? Where is my portion of bread?
I will not eat it for it is full of discontent, I will not drink the
blood of wrath which is given without mixture, but here I sit
and wait to be free.

Play it all by Ear

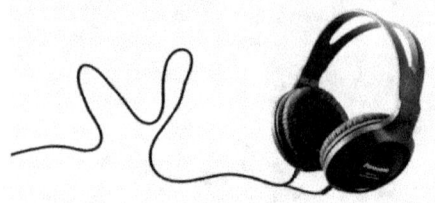

As I rage on in this world hard and cold it's not growing old
that I fear, it's not knowing my way, should I go? or just stay I
play it all by ear.

You tighten your grip around my throat but it's not death that I
fear ,
loosing again I just bare it and grin, I play it all by ear.

I lost all my fight I feel tired in the night ,the setting foreboding
and queer ,remember my name while you're playing your game
, I play it all by ear.

You took everything from me , your callous and mean so
what are you doing here ? I took it all back your fat lying sack,
because I play it all by ear.

Genuine

If you think that I can't write poems like this, I fully understand,
to find the right words a tedious challenge but on the other
hand.

The reason that I do this, with the clutter in my mind,
at times I'm only venting, not meant to be unkind.

I do it to feel like I belong, don't mistake me for weak,
I am not a carnival worker, or a 40's circus freak.

Be careful how you judge me, for I am just like you,
A starving poet whom loves to write I have to see it through.

This one is finally over so I'll leave you with this,
clap your hands, with no demands and blow my ass a kiss !!

<u>Grace</u>

grace
EPHESIANS 2:8

I've been down to hell below , third seat to the right the second
row ,
old friends were in torment crying out for mercy.

I was there a frightened man , my legs were to weak I couldn't
stand I thought that I was condemned and left to suffer.

All of the sudden I saw a light it was radiant and so was I ,
the peace that I felt just blew me away in that moment.

So if your lost cry out his name , he won't judge you nor will
he cast any blame , all of your sins and wrong doings can be
forgiven.

he knows your struggling , inside you're a mess , he sees your
heart hurting inside your chest , one at a time he will heal all
cuts and bruises.

So when your questioning your motives and faith, you need
to make some room on your plate, his love is always there for
those that choose it.

His Face

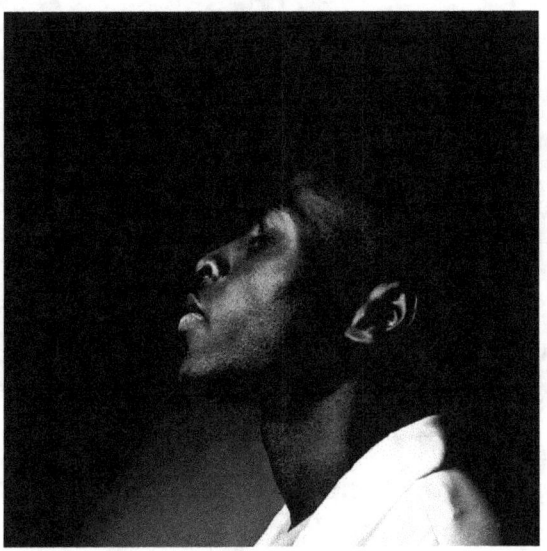

I have seen the most beautiful face, glowing with compassion ,
mercy and grace.
I could see he has power to forgive every sin ,I was just blown
away as I invited him in.
The love unlike anything I have known,
ever so humble with a spiritual tone he took a beating because
of men and their laws , willingly he did this, he believed in his
cause.

Someday we will see the whole, heavy, cost, the day he was
nailed to that old rugged cross and I will remember his face
forever.

<u>Crash</u>

Ever so gently your loving embrace engulfs me your sweet
breath is an opiate high
swimming in your waters, your scent drives me into
a frenzy.

I will drink from your well alone for a vow was made
I will meet your breast with a gentile caress ever so lightly I feel
the slip of your earlobe between my lips as I lay next to your
curves I lovingly kiss the nape of your
neck.

softly whispering my love for you and only you.

Truth

The truth is untarnished, the truth never lies, it needs no excuses
or cheap alibis.

The truth will expose every deed that is done,
for the thief and the liar it's a hot smoking gun.

the truth will set free those wrongly accused , the truth always
knows when it's just being used .
the truth can be a companion and friend , or it can come
crashing down and bring it all to an end.

So, search the truth in your heart and you just might see, that
you have been hurt and abused but now the truth set you free.

Man in Need

The woes of a poor man are only counted by him
his empty pockets constantly remind him of his plight
in his world he hasn't a well to draw from
who will help him in his time of need?

Remember when you also were in tatters , you held out your
hand and received your portion
consider the poor man's needs above your own
and discover your humanity and give.

One Thousand Faces

I cannot draw pictures but if I could , I would draw every detail
be they proper and good.

You would be amazed as you get lost in each curve ,
the bitter church lady would yell , you have some nerve !!!

But as it stands a face I can't draw , instead I write letters ,

if you read them all?

You may see faces , mountains and trees , or someone that is
dying from an unchecked disease.

Words retain power and the ones that I write
paint one thousand faces when their read in the light

Inspire

inspire

I will never judge you with hatred or disdain,
I will never cause you strife that you may in peace
remain.
God forbid anyone insult you or clip your angel wings ,
I will stand in awe of you and the wonder that you bring.
I will knock down all the walls and break the lock on the door
I will help you take the leap and watch your spirit soar
for you I wrote this insignificant poem to tell you of your worth
you will have your portion and your cup , you will be my friend
secure.

<u>Fight</u>

Do not be relaxed, be on your guard, do not be a fool .
for when we give in to strong drink we sin
and the demons sit laughing and drool.

In darkness we're lost such a steep heavy cost the rips and the
tares hard to mend,
so come to the light you may have to fight but I will
fight with you my friend.

<u>Shameless</u>

The pain you try to cover up deep inside your heart,
the abuse that you endured just ripped your world apart.
The anger that you cannot shake however hard you try.
Day by day it eats at you but doesn't tell you why.

Every day you mask your hurt afraid that someone just might
see,
I'm here to tell you Jesus does and longs to set you free.
Whatever it was that happened,
you are not to blame, the source of your unhappiness, your ill
unwanted shame.

Gently kneel and bow your head, open up your heart.
You don't have to change a thing
Jesus loves you just the way that you are.

<u>Wisdom</u>

The roads may be long and the mountains are steep, we pay a
price for the company we keep.
The lessons we learn lined with sorrow and pain, we wonder if
we'll ever be happy again.
you've been gone for a while the prodigal son, your inheritance
spent and your heart weighs a ton.

But the father rejoiced when he noticed his child, his arms
opened wide in his forgive my son style.
You see your place in his kingdom was there all along you may
have thought he'd be angry, thank God you were wrong.

**************END**************

www.ingramcontent.com/pod-product-compliance
Lightning Source LLC
Chambersburg PA
CBHW071002120626
46546CB00003B/887